D1088392

Discovery Biographies

Aviators
Amelia Earhart
Charles Lindbergh

**Conservationists
and Naturalists**
Rachel Carson

Educators
Mary McLeod Bethune
Booker T. Washington

Entertainers
Annie Oakley
The Ringling Brothers

Explorers
Juan Ponce de León
Marco Polo

First Ladies
Abigail Adams
Mary Todd Lincoln
Dolly Madison
Martha Washington

Government Leaders
Henry Clay

Military Heroes
David G. Farragut
Robert E. Lee
Paul Revere

Nurses and Doctors
Clara Barton
Elizabeth Blackwell
Florence Nightingale

**Pioneers and
Frontiersmen**
Jim Beckwourth
Daniel Boone
Jim Bridger
Davy Crockett
John Smith

Poets
Francis Scott Key

Presidents
Andrew Jackson
Abraham Lincoln
Harry S. Truman

**Engineers
and Inventors**
George W. Goethals
Samuel F. B. Morse
Eli Whitney

Social Reformers
Dorothea Dix
Frederick Douglass
Helen Keller

CHELSEA HOUSE PUBLISHERS

A Discovery Biography

Annie Oakley

—◆—

The Shooting Star

by Charles P. Graves
illustrated by Cary

CHELSEA JUNIORS
A division of Chelsea House Publishers
New York ◆ Philadelphia

For Liza to read to Granny

The Discovery Biographies have been prepared under the
educational supervision of Mary C. Austin, Ed.D.,
Reading Specialist and Professor of Education, Case
Western Reserve University.

Cover illustration: Maia Stone

First Chelsea House edition 1991

Copyright © MCMXCI by Chelsea House Publishers, a
division of Main Line Book Co. All rights reserved.
Printed and bound in the United States of America.
© MCMLXI by Charles P. Graves

5   7   9   8   6   4

ISBN   0-7910-1448-7

Contents

Annie Oakley: The Shooting Star

Chapter *1*

Thanksgiving Turkey

"Please let me shoot your gun, Father," seven-year old Phoebe Anne Moses begged.

It was the day before Thanksgiving. Annie had followed her stepfather into the forest. "If I ask him often enough," Annie thought, "he'll let me shoot."

"Annie," her stepfather said, "shooting is a man's job."

"Women used to shoot Indians right here in Ohio," Annie said. "Sometimes they had to when the men were away hunting. Lydia told me. She learned about it in school." Lydia was Annie's oldest sister.

Of course, there were no wild Indians in Ohio now. The year was 1867.

"All right, Annie," her stepfather agreed. "You win! You can shoot at the next game bird we see. When you miss," he laughed, "I'll try to hit it."

Annie's real father, Jacob Moses, had died when Annie was five. Her stepfather was named Dan Brumbaugh.

He was a good man. But he did not think that a girl belonged behind a gun. So he decided to play a trick on Annie. He felt sure the trick would cure her of wanting to shoot.

He put some extra powder in his gun. He knew this would make it kick extra hard. Of course, he did not want to hurt Annie. But he did want to make her afraid of a gun.

Suddenly they heard the "gobble, gobble" of a wild turkey. The big bird was just flying from the branch of a tree.

"Now's your chance, Annie," her stepfather said, handing her the gun.

Annie aimed carefully. When it felt right she pulled the trigger.

"BANG!" the gun roared. It was louder than usual because of the extra powder.

"OUCH!" cried Annie. The kick was much worse than her stepfather thought it would be. The butt of the gun slammed into Annie's face and shoulder.

"Oh, Annie, dear, I'm sorry," her stepfather cried. "I didn't mean to hurt you. I just meant to scare you a little."

Annie held back her tears. "I'm not sorry," she said. "I'm glad. Just look!"

Annie pointed to the turkey that was lying on the ground. She had shot it neatly in the head.

"Hooray!" she shouted. "We're going to have turkey for Thanksgiving!"

Her stepfather put his arm around her. "You're a good shot, Annie. I'm proud of you."

Together they walked home through the forest. Soon they reached the log cabin where they lived. Annie's mother met them at the door.

Mr. Brumbaugh held the turkey up for her to see. "Annie shot it," he said.

"How did you do it, Annie?" her mother asked.

"It was easy, Mother," Annie said. "When it felt right I just pulled the trigger."

For the rest of her life, shooting would be easy for Annie. She was on her way to becoming a shooting star.

Chapter *2*

Off to Work

The country near Greenville, Ohio, where Annie lived, was beautiful and wild. Annie loved to walk barefoot through the woods and fields. In the spring she climbed dogwood trees and picked the white flowers. She made a "queen's crown" out of dogwood flowers and wild roses.

"I'm a queen," Annie said to herself with a smile. "I'm the queen of . . . . I'm the queen of the woods, I guess." She never thought that someday she would meet real queens. Later, Annie was called "The Queen of the Rifle."

Annie did not have much time for play. She helped her mother with the housework. And she helped take care of Johnny and Hulda, her little brother and sister. Sometimes she fed the baby, Emily.

"Emily is my favorite doll," Annie said.

It was a busy and happy life. Sometimes Annie and Johnny built bird traps out of cornstalks. The birds they caught were good to eat.

But one day Annie's stepfather became sick. After a short time he died. It was a sad day for Annie and her family.

Annie's mother had very little money to buy food for her seven children. She got a job as a nurse, but it did not pay much. There was no one to take care of the children while she worked. So she sent the younger ones to stay with friends.

Annie went to live with Mr. and Mrs. Crawford Eddington. They had a home for orphans, children whose mothers and fathers had died. Mrs. Eddington taught Annie to sew. Annie often mended the children's clothes. And she helped in other ways.

Mrs. Eddington wanted to pay Annie for her work. But she did not have enough money.

One day a well-to-do farmer came to the home. He asked to speak to Mrs. Eddington. Annie showed him into the living room. She called Mrs. Eddington.

Annie left the room, but she stood close by the door. She knew she should not listen, but Annie had more curiosity than ten kittens.

"I'm looking for a girl to live with my family," the farmer told Mrs. Eddington. "I will pay her fifty cents a week. She won't have much work to do, and she can go to school."

Fifty cents is not much money today. But in those days it would buy a lot more than it does now.

Annie ran into the room. "Let me have the job," she cried. "I'll work hard."

"This is Annie Moses," Mrs. Eddington told the farmer. "She's only eight, but she's a hard worker."

"I'll pay you fifty cents each week," the farmer said.

"I don't want you to give me the money," Annie cried.

"My mother needs it very much. Please send it to her."

So Annie got the job. But it was not a good job for a little girl.

Chapter *3*

Escape

Annie rode in a wagon to the farmer's house. The farmer's wife met her at the front gate.

"I'd hoped we were going to get a bigger girl," she said to Annie. "You're going to have to work mighty hard."

"I'm willing to work hard," Annie said, standing on her toes so she would look taller. But Annie did not know what the woman meant by hard work.

The farmer's wife made Annie get up at four o'clock. First, Annie had to milk the cows and feed the pigs and chickens.

Then she had to build a fire in the stove and cook breakfast. Next, Annie pumped water, washed the dishes and dressed the baby. Then the woman made her sweep the house and scrub the kitchen floor. Annie never had any time to rest or play. And the farmer's wife would not let her go to school.

However, Annie did learn to ride a horse. She rode horseback when she brought the cows in from the fields to the barn. The only reason the farmer let Annie ride was because it saved time. That meant more time for her to do other chores.

On horseback Annie made a pretty picture. Her lovely brown hair flew in the wind.

"Riding is fun," Annie thought.

But that was all the fun Annie had. The farmer's wife scolded her many times a day.

Sometimes Annie was so tired that she almost fell asleep while working. Then she remembered that the farmer was sending money to her mother.

"I must stay awake," Annie said to herself. "Mother needs the money."

One night Annie heard the farmer talking to his wife.

"Annie is the biggest bargain we've ever had," he said.

"Aren't you sending money to her mother?" his wife asked.

"Of course not," Annie heard the farmer say. "Annie just thinks that I'm sending it. I wrote to her mother and said I could not pay Annie any money. But I told her Annie is happy with us and is going to school. Her mother wrote back. She said Annie could stay."

"Ha, ha!" the farmer's wife laughed. "You're a smart man. We must not let Annie know her mother isn't getting any money. Ha, ha, ha!"

Annie was angry. To think that she had worked so hard for nothing! She was afraid to say anything to the farmer or his wife. They would probably treat her even worse. And they might never let her go home.

That night, when Annie went to bed, she started to cry. But she soon fought back the tears.

"I must not cry," she thought. "I must plan to escape." Before she went to sleep Annie had made a plan.

The next night Annie went to bed with all her clothes on. She lay there quietly until she heard the farmer and his wife go to bed.

Soon she heard loud snoring from their room. Annie got up. She stuffed her pillow and an old blanket under the bed covers. If the farmer's wife looked in the room, she would think Annie was asleep in bed.

Annie tied her few belongings into a bundle. She started to tiptoe down the stairs.

"Creak!" Annie stepped on a loose board.

"What was that?" Annie heard the farmer's wife ask. "What was that noise?"

Annie froze in her tracks. Her heart seemed to beat as loudly as a drum. Surely they would hear it.

"That was a mouse," the farmer said to his wife. "Go back to sleep."

Annie could not help smiling. "I'm a pretty big mouse," she thought. "Now I must be quiet as a mouse."

She waited for the farmer and his wife to go back to sleep. Then she crept down the stairs and out of the house. When she reached the road, she started to run. There was a railroad station nearby. Annie planned to take the first train, no matter where it went.

Luckily, the first train went to a place near Annie's home. She climbed aboard.

"They can't catch me now," she said to herself. "I'll be home soon."

Chapter *4*

Quail for Sale

Annie was glad to see her mother. And her mother was really happy to see Annie. After they stopped hugging, Annie's mother told her some good news. She had just married again.

Annie's new stepfather was named Joseph Shaw. He was quite old. So the children called him "Grandpap Shaw." They loved him very much.

Grandpap Shaw bought a farm for Annie's mother and her children. He built a nice house for them. But he had to borrow money from the bank to pay for it.

It was hard for Mr. Shaw to earn enough money to pay the bank back. Annie wanted to help.

She started hunting again. She often shot birds, rabbits and squirrels for her family to eat. Her mother did not have to buy any meat. This saved money that could be used to help pay for the house.

Annie bought her shotgun shells from the general store in Greenville. It was run by Mr. Charles Katzenberger.

One day Annie brought a present to Mr. Katzenberger. The present was six fat birds, called quail. Annie knew that Mr. Katzenberger like to eat quail.

"Thank you, Annie," Mr. Katzenberger said. "You are a thoughtful girl. And, my," he cried, looking closely at the quail, "you're a mighty good shot."

"I try to hit them in the head," Annie said proudly. "That way no lead shots get in the meat. You could break a tooth off if you bit into a lead shot."

"That's right," Mr. Katzenberger agreed. "And that gives me an idea. I know a man who runs a hotel. He likes to serve quail in his dining room. He will pay good money for your quail."

"That's wonderful!" Annie cried. "I can shoot all the quail he can use. The money will help pay off the bank loan."

Every week, Annie brought quail to Mr. Katzenberger. He sent them to a hotel in Cincinnati. Because her quail were shot cleanly through the head, Annie got a big price. The hotel man knew his guests would not break their teeth on Annie's birds.

Annie gave most of the money she made to Grandpap Shaw. He paid it to the bank.

One day Grandpap came home from the bank and called Annie. "I made the last payment today," he said happily. "This house is now ours. Perhaps I should say, it's yours, Annie."

"Oh, no!" Annie cried. "*Ours* is the right word. We all own this house together."

Annie did not know it then, but she was not going to live in the house very long.

A few days later she had a letter from her oldest sister, Lydia. Lydia was now married to a man named Joe Stein. They lived in Cincinnati. Lydia asked Annie to come for a visit.

Annie shot quail for a few more weeks. When she had saved enough money, she bought a train ticket to Cincinnati.

Chapter *5*

Shooting Match

Cincinnati was the biggest city Annie had ever seen. Lydia and her husband, Joe, showed Annie many interesting places. They even took her to a shooting gallery. Annie hit the targets each time she shot.

"You're wonderful, Annie," Joe said. "There aren't many men who can shoot as well as you can."

"There's one man who can shoot better," Lydia said. "At least, he should shoot better. His name is Frank Butler. He does trick shooting at the Coliseum Theater."

"I bet Annie can outshoot him," Joe answered. "Annie," he asked, "will you have a shooting match with Frank Butler?"

"Sure," Annie said with a grin. "I'll try anything with a gun."

The match was held on Thanksgiving Day in 1876. The prize was fifty dollars. Annie surely wanted to win.

She did not eat much turkey that day. She wanted to be wide awake when she started shooting.

Annie met Frank Butler at the shooting grounds. They shook hands. Annie thought Frank was the most handsome man she had ever seen. He had a green feather in his cap.

"He looks like Yankee Doodle," Annie thought.

Frank Butler liked Annie too. "What a beautiful little lady!" he said. Annie was fifteen, but she was very short and always would be.

The targets used in the shooting match were called clay pigeons. The pigeons were really just round pieces of clay that looked like saucers.

When a shooter cried, "pull," a clay pigeon was sent flying up in the air. The shooter had to hit it before it touched the ground.

Frank Butler shot first.

"Pull," he cried. The pigeon sailed into the air.

"Bang!" went Frank's gun.

The clay pigeon was shattered.

"Dead!" cried the referee. He meant that Frank had hit the target.

Now it was Annie's turn. "It should be easier than hitting quail," she told herself. "When it feels right, I'll shoot."

"Pull!" she ordered. The clay saucer flew into the air.

"Bang!" Annie's gun spoke.

"Dead!" cried the referee. Annie had hit the target.

Both Frank and Annie had to shoot at twenty-five clay pigeons. The one that hit the most would win. Frank had a turn and hit his clay pigeon. Then Annie had a turn. She hit her pigeon. And so it went. It looked like the match might end in a tie.

Finally, on the twenty-fifth shot, Frank Butler missed. If Annie could hit the last pigeon, she would win.

"Pull!" Annie cried.

"Dead!" shouted the referee as Annie hit her pigeon.

The crowd cheered wildly. Annie had beaten the great Frank Butler. But Frank did not seem to mind. He went up to Annie and stuck out his hand.

"Well done, Miss Moses," he said. "I am proud to be beaten by such a good shot."

"Thank you, Mr. Butler," Annie said. "I hope we can have another match."

"I hope so too," Frank answered.

Just then Joe and Lydia rushed up to Annie.

"Come on," Joe cried. "Let's go get your fifty dollars!"

Chapter 6

On Stage

Frank Butler often said that he lost both the shooting match and his heart to Annie. And Annie said that she won the match and a husband.

Within a year Frank and Annie were married.

Frank had to be at the theater every night for his shooting act. He and his partner, Billy Graham, did many kinds of trick shooting.

They had a white-nosed poodle dog named George. At the end of the act, Billy placed an apple on George's head.

Then Frank aimed and shot the apple off the dog's head. This always brought loud clapping from the people watching.

Annie often clapped the loudest. She watched the show every night. After it was over, she went backstage to meet Frank.

One night Billy Graham became very sick just before the act was to begin. The theater was already full of people. Annie was there. Frank sent word for her to come backstage.

"Billy can't be my partner tonight," he said. "You'll have to take his place."

"But I have never been on a stage," Annie said.

"That's nothing. You've been watching every night. You know our act by heart. And you are a better shot than Billy."

When Annie walked out on the stage, the crowd roared with delight. She did all the trick shooting that Billy had done. When it was time to shoot the apple off George's head, Frank made Annie try it.

Annie raised her gun and aimed at the apple. She pulled the trigger. The apple burst into many small pieces. They were scattered about the stage. George started eating the bits of apple. The crowd laughed.

When the curtain fell, Frank said, "They loved you, Annie! From now on you're my partner on stage as well as at home. Together we can make lots of money. People like to see a girl shoot. Few girls shoot well."

"I like shooting on the stage," Annie said. "It's fun!"

"You must have a stage name," Frank said.

"What's wrong with Annie Butler?"

"Your name should be different from mine. Maybe Annie Moses will do."

"Oh, no," Annie cried. "My family wouldn't like me to use their name on the stage."

Frank and Annie talked about many last names. Finally they picked "Oakley." They liked the way "Annie Oakley" sounded.

And so Annie Moses Butler became Annie Oakley on the stage. As "Butler & Oakley" Annie and her husband became a popular shooting team. Wherever they went Annie was cheered by the crowds.

One day Frank and Annie gave their act before a group of cowboys in Texas.

For some reason Frank could not hit anything. He kept missing a trick shot that was supposed to be his best.

Annie felt sorry for Frank. But there was nothing she could do to help.

Suddenly, a big cowboy yelled, "Hey, Butler, get out of here and let the little girl shoot." The cowboy had a gun. It looked as if he might use it on Frank.

"Frank," Annie whispered. "Let me try the trick shot." Annie hit the target on her first try. The crowd cheered.

Later Frank said, "Annie, you're a better shot than I can ever be. It's you the people come to see."

"Now Frank," Annie said. "You were a famous shot long before we were married."

"But you are more famous than I am now," said Frank. "I'll be your manager. I'll take care of the business matters. You do the shooting. I'll throw your targets in the air."

"All right," Annie said. "But you are just as important on this team as I am. Don't ever forget that."

From that time on Annie did all the shooting. After one show the people voted Annie a queen. They named her "The Queen of the Rifle."

Chapter 7

Buffalo Bill's Show

One of the most famous buffalo hunters and Indian fighters in America was a man named William S. Cody. He was called "Buffalo Bill."

When he stopped fighting Indians, he started a Wild West Show. He wanted people in the eastern part of America to see what the West was really like.

The people who came to his show saw wild buffalo, deer, elk and bear. They saw Indians wearing war bonnets, the feathers trailing to the ground.

The show had cowboys who rode bucking horses. There were make-believe bandits who robbed a stage coach. The show also had some men who were good shooters.

Buffalo Bill met Annie and Frank in Kentucky. Annie was so small that Buffalo Bill did not believe she could shoot.

When she showed him how good she was with a gun, he changed his mind.

"I wish you'd been with me when I fought the Indians," Buffalo Bill said.

"Would you like me to be in your show?" Annie asked.

"You bet I would," Buffalo Bill said. "All the boys and girls in America will want to see you shoot."

So Annie, with Frank as her manager, joined Buffalo Bill's Wild West Show.

From the very start Buffalo Bill called her "Missie." So Annie got still another name.

Everybody liked Annie's act. She rode into the arena on a snow-white horse. Annie wore a buckskin skirt and shirt. Her chestnut hair flashed below her big cowboy hat. Her blue eyes shone with pleasure.

Frank threw some glass balls into the air. Annie, still on horseback, raised her gun.

"Crack!" With each shot Annie broke a glass ball.

Then Annie got off her horse. Frank held a coin between his thumb and forefinger. Annie shot the coin out of his fingers. Next Frank held up a playing card. Annie shot the spots out of it.

A wheel with lighted candles started to spin. Annie shot the flames and put the candles out.

The Wild West Show went to many cities. Annie was popular in all of them.

Years before, Buffalo Bill had fought against Sitting Bull, the great Sioux Indian chief. Now he and Sitting Bull were friends. Buffalo Bill asked Sitting Bull to join the Wild West show.

Sitting Bull looked more like a bird than a bull. He had a big beak-like nose and dark eyes. His chest was almost as big as a barrel.

When Sitting Bull saw Annie shoot, he grunted with pleasure. Annie reminded him of his own daughter who had died many years before. Sitting Bull came to Annie's tent.

"You are like my own daughter," he said. "But she has gone to the Happy Hunting Ground. Will you be my adopted daughter? I will make you a member of the Sioux tribe."

"Thank you," Annie said. "I've already had one real father and two stepfathers. I guess I can have one more father."

Sitting Bull lit his peace pipe. He blew a puff of smoke over Annie's head.

"I name you Wan-tan-yeya Ci-sci-la," Sitting Bull said. In the Sioux language that means "Little Sureshot."

That's the way Annie got still another name. Years later, when Sitting Bull died, he left all his possessions to his Little Sureshot. Among them were his moccasins, his peace pipe and his council stick.

Chapter 8

Kings and Queens

One night after a show in New York, Annie told Frank some exciting news.

"Buffalo Bill had a letter from Mark Twain today! Think of it—from Mark Twain!" Mark Twain was the famous author of *Tom Sawyer*.

"What did the letter say?" Frank asked.

"Mr. Twain said the Wild West Show should go to England. He said our show is real to the last detail. It will show people in England what the West is like."

One spring day in 1887, the Wild West Show sailed for England. The ship was named the *State of Nebraska*.

On board were more than two hundred cowboys, Indians and Mexicans. There were also many horses, buffalo, elk, deer, bear and antelope. Someone said the ship should be called *The Ark*.

It was a rough trip. Many cowboys and Indians were seasick, but Annie felt fine all the way.

When the ship sailed up the river to London, Annie and Frank were standing on deck. A tugboat, flying the American flag, came to welcome them.

The Prince and Princess of Wales came to see the show in London. Some day they would be King and Queen of England. The Prince was thrilled by Annie's trick shooting. He and the Princess came to see Annie after the show.

"I wish we had a thousand girls just like you in the English army," the Prince said. "You are the best shot in the world."

Later, Queen Victoria, the Prince's mother, came to the show. She brought some Kings and Queens who were visiting her from other countries.

Buffalo Bill, riding on his horse, led the grand parade. He was waving a large American flag. Behind him, on their horses came the cowboys and Indians. The Indians were colorful in their feathered headdresses and war paint. The cowboys and Indians broke the silence with yells and war whoops.

The whole company lined up behind Buffalo Bill before the Queen. The cowboys held their hats high in the air.

The Queen stood up. Then she bowed her head to the American flag.

"Yi-peeee!" the cowboys screamed. Their yells could be heard for miles. It was a wonderful thing for the Queen to do.

The Queen sat down. Buffalo Bill and the cowboys and Indians left.

Suddenly, Annie Oakley galloped in. The spotlights followed her to the center of the ring.

Her helper threw three glass balls into the air.

"Bang! Bang! Bang!" Annie hit them all.

Next Annie jumped from her horse. Five more glass balls were thrown high above her head. Annie quickly turned a handspring. She jumped over a table. Then she grabbed a gun and broke the glass balls before they hit the ground.

The cheers were deafening. Annie bowed to the crowd and left.

Then a herd of buffalo, chased by cowboys, ran into the ring.

After the show, Annie met Queen Victoria. Her son, Prince Edward, was standing beside her. The Queen asked Annie how old she was when she learned to shoot. Annie told her. The Queen said, "You are a very clever little girl."

"Thank you, your Majesty," Annie said politely.

A young Lord spoke to Annie. "Don't you feel nervous shooting before kings and queens?"

"Why no," Annie answered, giving him a friendly smile.

"I have shot before thousands of American boys and girls."

The Lord blushed, but the Prince laughed. He knew it was Annie's way of saying that she thought American boys and girls were just as important as kings and queens.

Annie was very popular in England. Four men asked her to marry them. People did not know she had a husband, for she used the name "Annie Oakley" instead of Mrs. Frank Butler.

One man sent Annie his picture. He said he wanted to marry her. Annie thought it was funny. She used the picture for a target. She shot several holes through the picture of the man's head. Then she sent the picture back to him.

When she told Frank, he roared with laughter. "That will teach him to leave my Annie alone," he said happily.

Chapter 9

A Diamond Pin

After the show closed in London, Annie and Frank went to Germany. Annie had been invited to shoot before the German king who was called the Kaiser.

A big crowd came to see Annie shoot. Then a message arrived from the Kaiser. He was too sick to come. This made the crowd sad. Annie was disappointed too.

At first the crowd watched her shooting in icy silence. Annie hit target after target. Slowly, the ice began to melt. Annie hit six targets that were thrown in the air at once.

The crowd clapped loudly. Prince William, the Kaiser's grandson, walked up to Annie.

"Miss Oakley," he said, "In London, you shot the ashes off a cigarette. It was held in your helper's mouth."

"That's right," Annie said.

"I would like you to do that trick here," the Prince said. "I will be your helper."

What could Annie do? She hated to refuse the Prince. What if she missed the cigarette and hit the Prince in the head?

Before she could think of an excuse, the Prince lit a cigarette. He held it between his lips. Annie swung her gun to her shoulder and took careful aim. Then she pulled the trigger. The ashes on the Prince's cigarette fell to the ground.

The crowd cheered for a long time.

After leaving Germany, Annie and Frank came back to America. Annie did trick shooting in the Wild West Show for many more years. She went back to Europe with the Wild West Show. They travelled in France and other countries.

Once Annie was in Vienna. A rich Baroness asked her to give a show to raise money to help some orphans. Annie remembered the orphans she knew when she lived with the Eddingtons. She was glad to help the Baroness raise money for the children.

Annie's show for the orphans in Vienna was a big success. A lot of money was raised. To thank Annie, the Baroness sent her a bag full of gold coins. Annie gave the gold coins to the orphans.

The Baroness soon heard about Annie's gift to the orphans. She was so pleased that she sent Annie a big diamond pin. The pin sparkled like fire when Annie wore it.

Chapter **10**

Annie's Last Show

One night in 1901, Annie and Frank were on the Wild West Show train. It was going from Charlotte, North Carolina, to Danville, Virginia.

Annie and Frank were sound asleep. Suddenly, they were awakened by a terrible crash.

"Are you all right, Annie?" Frank yelled.

"I think so, Frank," Annie answered.

The show train had hit a freight train. Both trains were wrecked. Nearly all the Wild West Show horses were killed. No people died, but many were hurt.

And Annie was not "all right." She was badly hurt. She had to wear a brace on her right leg for a long time.

Annie had to leave the Wild West Show. She and Frank bought a house in Nutley, New Jersey.

Everyone who had seen the Wild West Show when Annie was in it missed her.

A newspaper man reported, *"Where, oh, where is Annie Oakley? It does not seem quite the same old shooting match without Miss Oakley potting pigeons in the ring."*

Annie did not know if she would ever be able to shoot again. One day she took her gun and went into the woods. Frank and their dog went with her. Annie was still on crutches. But she wanted to see if she could still shoot.

Frank threw a coin into the air. Annie raised her gun to her shoulder. When it "felt right" she pulled the trigger.

"Ping!" the coin rang when Annie hit it. She was still "Little Sureshot."

Annie started giving shooting shows again. She also taught other people how to shoot. She loved to teach children.

When America was at war with Germany, Annie wanted to join the Army. She probably would have made a good soldier. But she knew the Army could not take an old lady.

However, Annie did help win the war. She visited many Army training camps. Annie showed young soldiers how easy shooting was.

"If I can shoot," Annie said, "you boys can shoot."

Finally, the war was over. Many American soldiers had been killed and hurt. Annie was asked to help raise money for those who returned. People would still pay to see her shoot.

"I'm afraid I can't shoot like I used to," Annie said. "But I am willing to try."

People who saw her said she had never been better. Frank Butler swung a ball on a cord around his head. Annie held her gun in her left hand. With her back toward Frank, she took aim in a mirror held in her right hand. She pulled the trigger. The bullet cut the cord. The ball sailed away.

Next, Annie leaned backwards over a chair and tossed three glass balls over her head. She grabbed a gun and broke each ball to bits.

"Hurrah for Annie Oakley," the crowd screamed. The next day, a newspaper said, "Miss Annie Oakley was the hit of the afternoon." Annie had hit just about everything with her gun.

Annie Oakley was still the shooting star. But her long, exciting life was near its end. Two years later, in 1926, Annie died quietly at the home of a friend in Ohio.

Like a shooting star in the sky, Annie's light went out.